SPOT

FEELINGS

ANGRY

by Alissa Thielges

scowl

throw

Look for these words and pictures as you read.

crossed arms

yell

Anger is a strong feeling.
It means you feel mad.

scowl

Lola is angry.
Her sister took her toy.
She scowls.

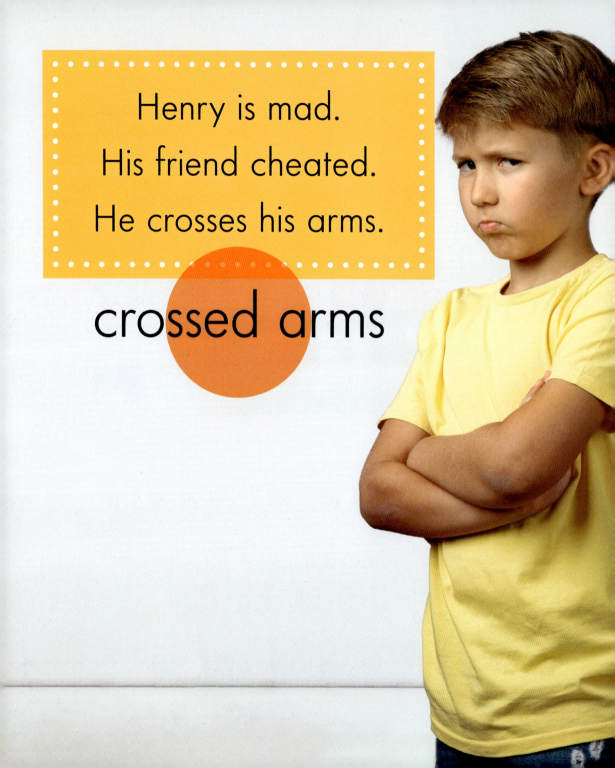

throw

Brock gets angry easily.
He lost a game.
He throws his toy.

Everyone gets mad sometimes. Take deep breaths.

You can talk about your anger. What makes you mad?

Spot is published by Amicus Learning, an imprint of Amicus
P.O. Box 227, Mankato, MN 56002
www.amicuspublishing.us

Copyright © 2025 Amicus.
International copyright reserved in all countries.
No part of this book may be reproduced in any form
without written permission from the publisher.

Names: Thielges, Alissa, 1995– author.
Title: Angry / by Alissa Thielges.
Description: Mankato, MN : Amicus Learning, [2025] | Series: Spot feelings | Audience: Ages 4–7 | Audience: Grades K-1 | Summary: "What makes kids feel angry? Encourage social-emotional learning with this beginning reader that introduces vocabulary for discussing feelings of anger with an engaging search-and-find feature"– Provided by publisher.
Identifiers: LCCN 2024017551 (print) | LCCN 2024017552 (ebook) | ISBN 9798892000789 (library binding) | ISBN 9798892001366 (paperback) | ISBN 9798892001946 (ebook)
Subjects: LCSH: Jealousy in children—Juvenile literature. | Jealousy—Juvenile literature.
Classification: LCC BF723.J4 B33 2025 (print) | LCC BF723.J4 (ebook) | DDC 152.4/8–dc23/eng/20240502
LC record available at https://lccn.loc.gov/2023039320
LC ebook record available at https://lccn.loc.gov/2023039321

Printed in China

Ana Brauer, editor
Deb Miner, series designer
Kim Pfeffer, book designer
and photo researcher

Photos by Alamy Stock Photo/Eloisa Ramos, 8; Freepik/freepik, 1, 7, 14, master1305, 3, user23778514, 6; Getty Images/georgeclerk, 8–9, kool99, 12–13, ktmoffitt, 11; Shutterstock/kornnphoto, 4–5, PeopleImages.com - Yuri A, cover